WRIGHT
Residences
for America

Drawings from the
Wasmuth (1910)
and American
System-Built
(1915–1917) Folios

A Book of Postcards
Library of Congress

Pomegranate Artbooks ☐ San Francisco

Pomegranate Artbooks
Box 6099
Rohnert Park, CA 94927

ISBN 0-87654-100-7
Pomegranate Catalog No. A757

Pomegranate publishes books of postcards on a wide range of subjects.
Please write to the publisher for more information.

Designed by Thomas Morley

Title page: Perspective, house for Mrs. Martin, Oak Park, Illinois, 1901.

Printed in Korea

06 05 04 03 02 01 00 99 98 97   11 10 9 8 7 6 5 4 3

This book of postcards presents thirty elegant architectural drawings by American architect Frank Lloyd Wright (1867–1959). Half are designs selected from *Ausgeführte Bauten und Entwürfe von Frank Lloyd Wright (Studies and Executed Buildings by Frank Lloyd Wright)*, a rare and prized collection of Wright's drawings published in 1910 by the distinguished German architectural publisher Ernst Wasmuth. Drawings in this folio emphasize Wright's Prairie Style buildings (characterized by low horizontal lines and projecting eaves and blending with the rhythms of the surrounding prairie landscape), one of the most outstanding of which is the Robie house, in Chicago (Plate XXXVII). The Wasmuth drawings earned Wright a solid reputation in Europe and greatly influenced architects of the day.

Also included are examples of Wright's "American System-Built Houses," designs he executed for The Richards Company of Milwaukee, Wisconsin, between 1915 and 1917. These designs were for prefabricated housing and, as such, are a very early documentation of Wright's lifelong preoccupation with the issue of affordable housing in America.

The original delineations for the American System-Built Houses were done in the style of Japanese woodblock prints. Most of the perspective, floor plan and interior plates include legends done in Wright's characteristic lettering and bearing his signature "chop" with vermilion accents. It is interesting to note that three perspectives are depicted twice, once with lettering and once without, and are on different papers. Each set evidences subtle differences in detail and shadowing and, in one case, in the cropping of the image. Graphically evocative, these housing designs echo Wright's mature Prairie House period residences.

Evidence is accumulating that The Richards Company built quite a few houses based on the Frank Lloyd Wright American System-Built designs. One has recently come to light on Chicago's south side, and research continues on several others thought to be Frank Lloyd Wright–Richards Company homes.

Together, the drawings from these two folios provide a beautiful and informative sampling of Wright's Prairie Style designs. All are from the Architecture, Design and Engineering Collections in the Prints and Photographs Division of the Library of Congress.

GEDRUCKT UND VERLEGT VON ERNST WASMUTH A.-G., BERLIN

DER TYPISCHE GRUNDRISS

FRANK LLOYD WRIGHT: Residences for America

Frank Lloyd Wright (American, 1867–1959)
Plate V. Perspective, plan and detail, Francis Apartments,
Forestville Avenue and 32nd Street, Chicago, 1893.
Adapted from the Frank Lloyd Wright drawing as originally
published in *Ausgeführte Bauten und Entwürfe von Frank
Lloyd Wright* (*Studies and Executed Buildings by Frank
Lloyd Wright*) by Verlag Ernst Wasmuth A.G., Berlin, 1910.

Pomegranate, Box 6099, Rohnert Park, CA 94927

GEDRUCKT UND VERLEGT VON ERNST WASMUTH A.-G., BERLIN

FRANK LLOYD WRIGHT: Residences for America

Frank Lloyd Wright (American, 1867–1959)
Plate XIII. Perspective, typical house in the "Quadruple
Block Plan," a variation on the usual American city block.
Adapted from the Frank Lloyd Wright drawing as originally
published in *Ausgeführte Bauten und Entwürfe von Frank
Lloyd Wright* (*Studies and Executed Buildings by Frank
Lloyd Wright*) by Verlag Ernst Wasmuth A.G., Berlin, 1910.

Pomegranate, Box 6099, Rohnert Park, CA 94927

GEDRUCKT UND VERLEGT VON ERNST WASMUTH A.-G., BERLIN

FRANK LLOYD WRIGHT: Residences for America

Frank Lloyd Wright (American, 1867–1959)
Plate XV. Perspective, Thomas P. Hardy house, Racine, Wisconsin.
Adapted from the Frank Lloyd Wright drawing as originally published in *Ausgeführte Bauten und Entwürfe von Frank Lloyd Wright* (*Studies and Executed Buildings by Frank Lloyd Wright*) by Verlag Ernst Wasmuth A.G., Berlin, 1910.

Pomegranate, Box 6099, Rohnert Park, CA 94927

GEDRUCKT UND VERLEGT VON ERNST WASMUTH A.-G., BERLIN

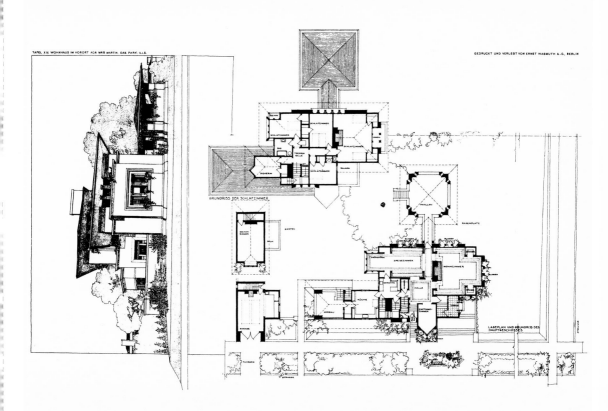

GRUNDRISS DER SCHLAFZIMMER.

LAGEPLAN UND GRUNDRISS DES
HAUPTGESCHOSSES

FRANK LLOYD WRIGHT: Residences for America

Frank Lloyd Wright (American, 1867–1959)
Plate XIX. Perspective and plan, house for Mrs. Martin, Oak
Park, Illinois, 1901.
Adapted from the Frank Lloyd Wright drawing as originally
published in *Ausgeführte Bauten und Entwürfe von Frank
Lloyd Wright* (*Studies and Executed Buildings by Frank
Lloyd Wright*) by Verlag Ernst Wasmuth A.G., Berlin, 1910.

Pomegranate, Box 6099, Rohnert Park, CA 94927

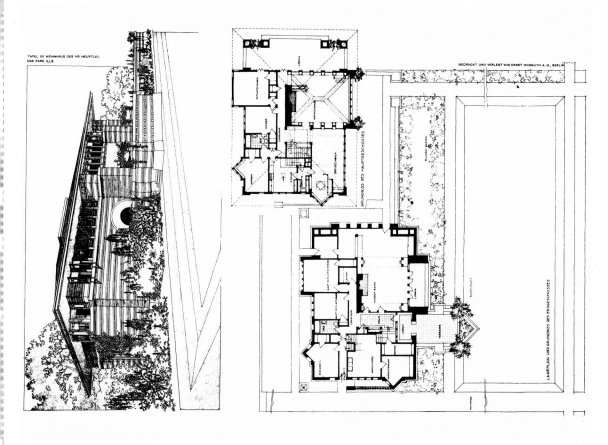

TAFEL XX WOHNHAUS DES HR. HEURTLEY,
OAK PARK, ILLS.

GEDRUCKT UND VERLEGT VON ERNST WASMUTH A.-G., BERLIN

GRUNDRISS DES HAUPTGESCHOSSES

LAGEPLAN UND GRUNDRISS DES ERDGESCHOSSES

FRANK LLOYD WRIGHT: Residences for America

Frank Lloyd Wright (American, 1867–1959)
Plate XX. Perspective and plan, house for Arthur Heurtley,
Oak Park, Illinois.
Adapted from the Frank Lloyd Wright drawing as originally
published in *Ausgeführte Bauten und Entwürfe von Frank
Lloyd Wright* (*Studies and Executed Buildings by Frank
Lloyd Wright*) by Verlag Ernst Wasmuth A.G., Berlin, 1910.

Pomegranate, Box 6099, Rohnert Park, CA 94927

GEDRUCKT UND VERLEGT VON ERNST WASMUTH A.-G. BERLIN

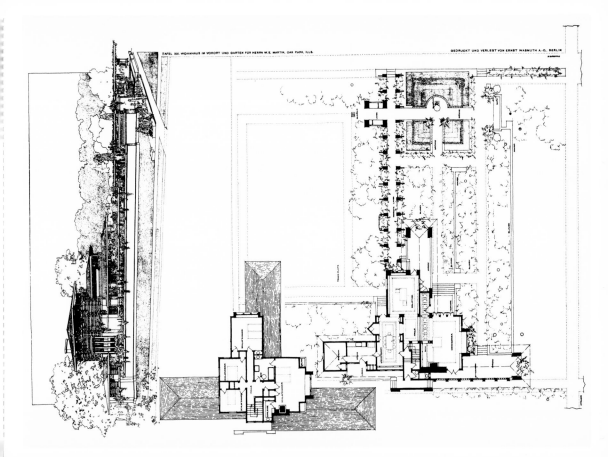

FRANK LLOYD WRIGHT: Residences for America

Frank Lloyd Wright (American, 1867–1959)
Plate XXI. Perspective and plan, house and garden for
W. E. Martin, Oak Park, Illinois.
Adapted from the Frank Lloyd Wright drawing as originally
published in *Ausgeführte Bauten und Entwürfe von Frank
Lloyd Wright* (*Studies and Executed Buildings by Frank
Lloyd Wright*) by Verlag Ernst Wasmuth A.G., Berlin, 1910.

Pomegranate, Box 6099, Rohnert Park, CA 94927

GEDRUCKT UND VERLEGT VON ERNST WASMUTH A.-G. BERLIN

FRANK LLOYD WRIGHT: Residences for America

Frank Lloyd Wright (American, 1867–1959)
Plate XXII. Interior perspective, living room of Harley
Bradley house, Kankakee, Illinois.
Adapted from the Frank Lloyd Wright drawing as originally
published in *Ausgeführte Bauten und Entwürfe von Frank
Lloyd Wright* (*Studies and Executed Buildings by Frank
Lloyd Wright*) by Verlag Ernst Wasmuth A.G., Berlin, 1910.

Pomegranate, Box 6099, Rohnert Park, CA 94927

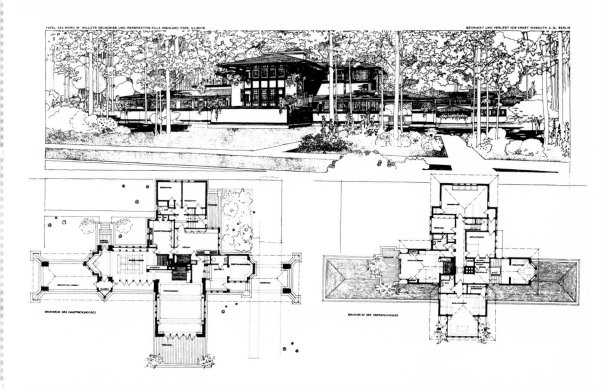

GRUNDRISS DES HAUPTGESCHOSSES

GRUNDRISS DES OBERGESCHOSSES

FRANK LLOYD WRIGHT: Residences for America

Frank Lloyd Wright (American, 1867–1959)
Plate XXV. Perspective and plan, Ward W. Willitt house,
Highland Park, Illinois.
Adapted from the Frank Lloyd Wright drawing as originally
published in *Ausgeführte Bauten und Entwürfe von Frank
Lloyd Wright* (*Studies and Executed Buildings by Frank
Lloyd Wright*) by Verlag Ernst Wasmuth A.G., Berlin, 1910.

Pomegranate, Box 6099, Rohnert Park, CA 94927

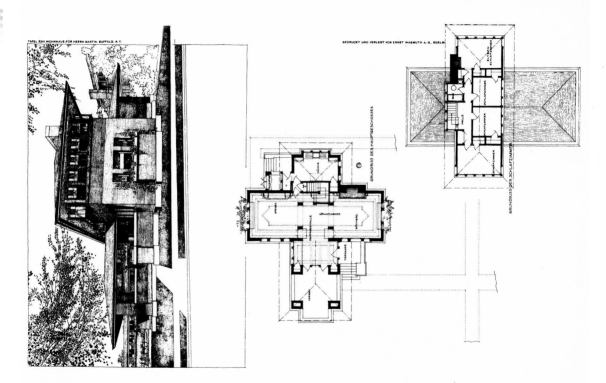

GEDRUCKT UND VERLEGT VON ERNST WASMUTH A.-G., BERLIN

GRUNDRISS DES HAUPTGESCHOSSES

GRUNDRISS DER SCHLAFZIMMER

FRANK LLOYD WRIGHT: Residences for America

Frank Lloyd Wright (American, 1867–1959)
Plate XXVI. Perspective and plan, masonry house for Mr.
Martin, Buffalo, New York.
Adapted from the Frank Lloyd Wright drawing as originally
published in *Ausgeführte Bauten und Entwürfe von Frank
Lloyd Wright* (*Studies and Executed Buildings by Frank
Lloyd Wright*) by Verlag Ernst Wasmuth A.G., Berlin, 1910.

Pomegranate, Box 6099, Rohnert Park, CA 94927

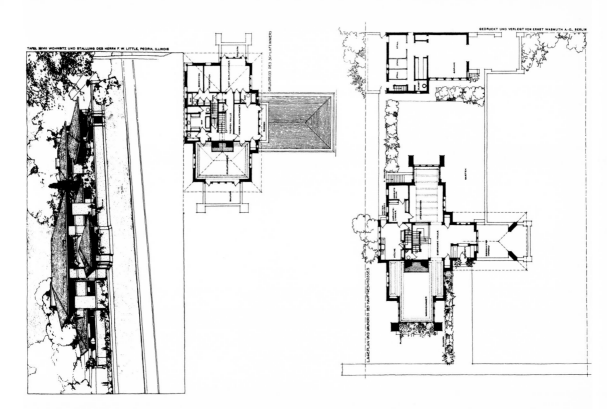

TAFEL XXVIII WOHNSITZ UND STALLUNG DES HERRN F. W. LITTLE, PEORIA, ILLINOIS

GRUNDRISS DES SCHLAFZIMMERS

LAGEPLAN UND GRUNDRISS DES HAUPTGESCHOSSES

FRANK LLOYD WRIGHT: Residences for America

Frank Lloyd Wright (American, 1867–1959)
Plate XXVIII. Perspective and plan, house for F. W. Little,
Peoria, Illinois, 1900.
Adapted from the Frank Lloyd Wright drawing as originally
published in *Ausgeführte Bauten und Entwürfe von Frank
Lloyd Wright* (*Studies and Executed Buildings by Frank
Lloyd Wright*) by Verlag Ernst Wasmuth A.G., Berlin, 1910.

Pomegranate, Box 6099, Rohnert Park, CA 94927

GEDRUCKT UND VERLEGT VON ERNST WASMUTH A.-G. BERLIN

FRANK LLOYD WRIGHT: Residences for America

Frank Lloyd Wright (American, 1867–1959)
Plate XXX. Perspective, house for E. H. Cheney, Oak Park, Illinois, 1904.
Adapted from the Frank Lloyd Wright drawing as originally published in *Ausgeführte Bauten und Entwürfe von Frank Lloyd Wright* (*Studies and Executed Buildings by Frank Lloyd Wright*) by Verlag Ernst Wasmuth A.G., Berlin, 1910.

Pomegranate, Box 6099, Rohnert Park, CA 94927

GEDRUCKT UND VERLEGT VON ERNST WASMUTH A.-G. BERLIN

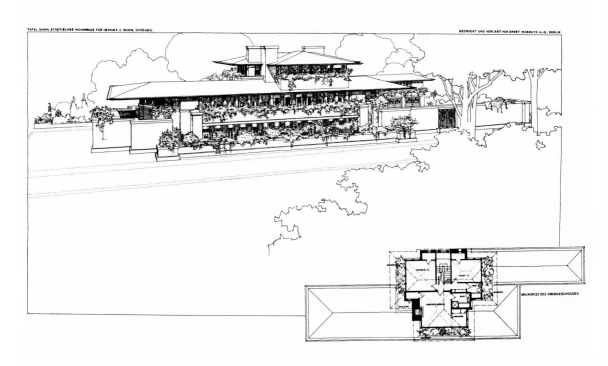

GRUNDRISS DES OBERGESCHOSSES

FRANK LLOYD WRIGHT: Residences for America

Frank Lloyd Wright (American, 1867–1959)
Plate XXXVII. Perspective and plan, house for Fred C.
Robie, Woodlawn Avenue and 57th Street, Chicago, 1909.
Adapted from the Frank Lloyd Wright drawing as originally
published in *Ausgeführte Bauten und Entwürfe von Frank
Lloyd Wright* (*Studies and Executed Buildings by Frank
Lloyd Wright*) by Verlag Ernst Wasmuth A.G., Berlin, 1910.

Pomegranate, Box 6099, Rohnert Park, CA 94927

GEDRUCKT UND VERLEGT VON ERNST WASMUTH A.-G., BERLIN

FRANK LLOYD WRIGHT: Residences for America

Frank Lloyd Wright (American, 1867–1959)
Plate XLIV. Perspective and plan, house for George E.
Millard, Highland Park, Illinois.
Adapted from the Frank Lloyd Wright drawing as originally
published in *Ausgeführte Bauten und Entwürfe von Frank
Lloyd Wright* (*Studies and Executed Buildings by Frank
Lloyd Wright*) by Verlag Ernst Wasmuth A.G., Berlin, 1910.

Pomegranate, Box 6099, Rohnert Park, CA 94927

GEDRUCKT UND VERLEGT VON ERNST WASMUTH A.-G., BERLIN

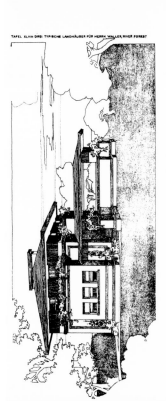

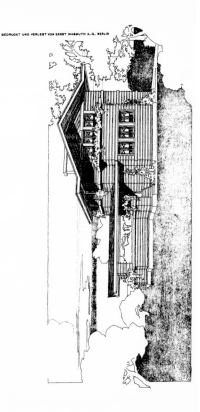

FRANK LLOYD WRIGHT: Residences for America

Frank Lloyd Wright (American, 1867–1959)
Plate XLVIII. Perspectives, three typical houses for a real
estate subdivision for E. C. Waller.
Adapted from the Frank Lloyd Wright drawing as originally
published in *Ausgeführte Bauten und Entwürfe von Frank
Lloyd Wright* (*Studies and Executed Buildings by Frank
Lloyd Wright*) by Verlag Ernst Wasmuth A.G., Berlin, 1910.

Pomegranate, Box 6099, Rohnert Park, CA 94927

GEDRUCKT UND VERLEGT VON ERNST WASMUTH A.-G., BERLIN

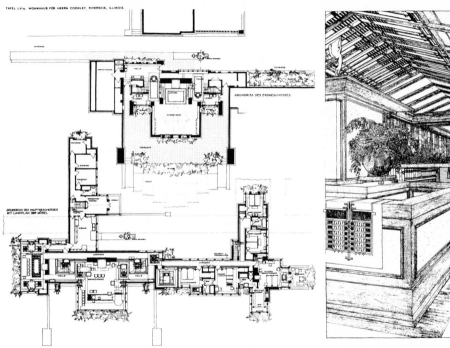

GRUNDRISS DES ERDGESCHOSSES

GRUNDRISS DES HAUPTGESCHOSSES
MIT LAGEPLAN DER MÖBEL

FRANK LLOYD WRIGHT: Residences for America

Frank Lloyd Wright (American, 1867–1959)
Plate LVIa. Plan and interior perspective, house for Mr. and Mrs. Avery Coonley, Riverside, Illinois.
Adapted from the Frank Lloyd Wright drawing as originally published in *Ausgeführte Bauten und Entwürfe von Frank Lloyd Wright* (*Studies and Executed Buildings by Frank Lloyd Wright*) by Verlag Ernst Wasmuth A.G., Berlin, 1910.

Pomegranate, Box 6099, Rohnert Park, CA 94927

AMERICAN·MODEL·J902·PATENTS
APPLIED·FOR
AMERICAN·SYSTEM-BUILT
HOUSES□DESIGNED·BY
FRANK·LLOYD·WRIGHT
THE·RICHARDS·COMPANY
PROPRIETORS·MILWAUKEE

FRANK LLOYD WRIGHT: Residences for America

Frank Lloyd Wright (American, 1867–1959)
Perspective, American Model J902. One of a series of
American System-Built Houses designed for The Richards
Company, Milwaukee, Wisconsin.

Pomegranate, Box 6099, Rohnert Park, CA 94927

FRANK LLOYD WRIGHT: Residences for America

Frank Lloyd Wright (American, 1867–1959)
Perspective, one of a series of American System-Built
Houses designed for The Richards Company, Milwaukee,
Wisconsin.

Pomegranate, Box 6099, Rohnert Park, CA 94927

AMERICAN·MODEL·D1□ ·PATENTS□□
AMERICAN·SYSTEM·BUILT ·APPLIED·FOR
HOUSES□ ·DESIGNED·BY
FRANK·LLOYD·WRIGHT □
THE·RICHARDS·COMPANY
PROPRIETORS·MILWAUKEE

FRANK LLOYD WRIGHT: Residences for America

Frank Lloyd Wright (American, 1867–1959)
Perspective, American Model D1. One of a series of
American System-Built Houses designed for The Richards
Company, Milwaukee, Wisconsin.

Pomegranate, Box 6099, Rohnert Park, CA 94927

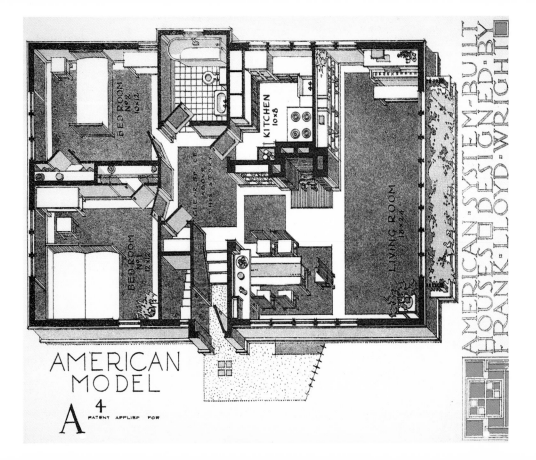

BED ROOM
No 2
10×12

KITCHEN
10×8

CLEAR SPACE
ABOVE
THIS STORY

BED ROOM
No 1
12×12

LIVING ROOM
13×24

AMERICAN
MODEL

A⁴
PATENT APPLIED FOR

AMERICAN·SYSTEM·BUILT
HOUSES□DESIGNED·BY
FRANK·LLOYD·WRIGHT·

FRANK LLOYD WRIGHT: **Residences for America**

Frank Lloyd Wright (American, 1867–1959)
Plan, American Model A4. One of a series of American
System-Built Houses designed for The Richards Company,
Milwaukee, Wisconsin.

Pomegranate, Box 6099, Rohnert Park, CA 94927

AMERICAN · MODEL · D101 · PATENTS ☐☐
APPLIED · FOR
AMERICAN · SYSTEM·BUILT
HOUSES ☐ DESIGNED · BY
FRANK·LLOYD·WRIGHT ☐
THE·RICHARDS·COMPANY
PROPRIETORS·MILWAUKEE

FRANK LLOYD WRIGHT: Residences for America

Frank Lloyd Wright (American, 1867–1959)
Perspective, American Model D101. One of a series of
American System-Built Houses designed for The Richards
Company, Milwaukee, Wisconsin.

Pomegranate, Box 6099, Rohnert Park, CA 94927

FRANK LLOYD WRIGHT: Residences for America

Frank Lloyd Wright (American, 1867–1959)
Perspective, one of a series of American System-Built
Houses designed for The Richards Company, Milwaukee,
Wisconsin.

Pomegranate, Box 6099, Rohnert Park, CA 94927

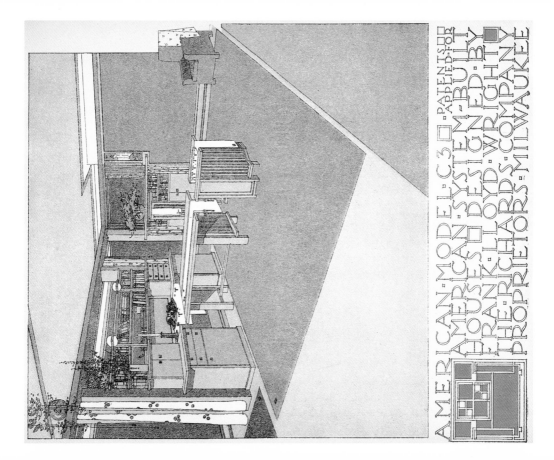

AMERICAN·MODEL·C3□ □·APPLIED·FOR
PATENTS□
AMERICAN·SYSTEM·BUILT·
HOUSES□ DESIGNED·BY·
FRANK·LLOYD·WRIGHT□
THE·RICHARDS·COMPANY·
PROPRIETORS·MILWAUKEE

FRANK LLOYD WRIGHT: Residences for America

Frank Lloyd Wright (American, 1867–1959)
Interior perspective, American Model C3. One of a series
of American System-Built Houses designed for The
Richards Company, Milwaukee, Wisconsin.

Pomegranate, Box 6099, Rohnert Park, CA 94927

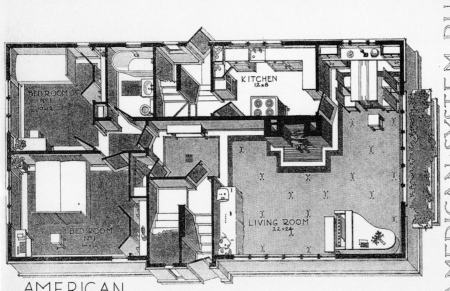

KITCHEN
12×8

BED ROOM
No. 2
10×12

BED ROOM
No. 1
14×12

LIVING ROOM
22×24

AMERICAN
MODEL
J 400
PATENT APPLIED FOR

AMERICAN·SYSTEM·BUILT
HOUSES·DESIGNED·BY
FRANK·LLOYD·WRIGHT
THE·RICHARDS·COMPANY
PROPRIETORS·MILWAUKEE

FRANK LLOYD WRIGHT: Residences for America

Frank Lloyd Wright (American, 1867–1959)
Plan, American Model J400. One of a series of American
System-Built Houses designed for The Richards Company,
Milwaukee, Wisconsin.

Pomegranate, Box 6099, Rohnert Park, CA 94927

AMERICAN·MODEL·J401·PATENTS□□
AMERICAN·SYSTEM·BUILT·□·APPLIED·FOR
HOUSES□·DESIGNED·BY
FRANK·LLOYD·WRIGHT·■
THE·RICHARDS·COMPANY
PROPRIETORS·MILWAUKEE

FRANK LLOYD WRIGHT: Residences for America

Frank Lloyd Wright (American, 1867–1959)
Perspective, American Model J401. One of a series of
American System-Built Houses designed for The Richards
Company, Milwaukee, Wisconsin.

Pomegranate, Box 6099, Rohnert Park, CA 94927

FRANK LLOYD WRIGHT: Residences for America

Frank Lloyd Wright (American, 1867–1959)
Perspective, American Model D101. One of a series of
American System-Built Houses designed for The Richards
Company, Milwaukee, Wisconsin.

Pomegranate, Box 6099, Rohnert Park, CA 94927

AMERICAN·MODEL·E3 □ □ PATENTS □
AMERICAN·SYSTEM·BUILT □ APPLIED·FOR
HOUSES □ DESIGNED·BY
FRANK·LLOYD·WRIGHT □
THE·RICHARDS·COMPANY
PROPRIETORS·MILWAUKEE

FRANK LLOYD WRIGHT: Residences for America

Frank Lloyd Wright (American, 1867–1959)
Perspective, American Model E3. One of a series of
American System-Built Houses designed for The Richards
Company, Milwaukee, Wisconsin.

Pomegranate, Box 6099, Rohnert Park, CA 94927

FRANK LLOYD WRIGHT: Residences for America

Frank Lloyd Wright (American, 1867–1959)
Perspective, American Model E3. One of a series of
American System-Built Houses designed for The Richards
Company, Milwaukee, Wisconsin.

Pomegranate, Box 6099, Rohnert Park, CA 94927

AMERICAN·MODEL·A231 ·PATENTS·
·APPLIED·FOR
AMERICAN·SYSTEM-BUILT
HOUSES □ DESIGNED·BY
FRANK·LLOYD·WRIGHT□
THE·RICHARDS·COMPANY
PROPRIETORS·MILWAUKEE

FRANK LLOYD WRIGHT: Residences for America

Frank Lloyd Wright (American, 1867–1959)
Perspective, American Model A231. One of a series of
American System-Built Houses designed for The Richards
Company, Milwaukee, Wisconsin.

Pomegranate, Box 6099, Rohnert Park, CA 94927

FRANK LLOYD WRIGHT: Residences for America

Frank Lloyd Wright (American, 1867–1959)
Perspective, American Model J902. One of a series of
American System-Built Houses designed for The Richards
Company, Milwaukee, Wisconsin.

Pomegranate, Box 6099, Rohnert Park, CA 94927